FINISHING LINE PRESS

www.finishinglinepress.com

Un-

poems by

Laurel Blossom

Finishing Line Press
Georgetown, Kentucky

Un-

ACKNOWLEDGMENTS

These poems were published in *Taos Journal of International Poetry & Art #3*
(online): "Mansion on the Beach" and "In Marion Davies's Pool."

Publisher: Leah Maines
Editor: Christen Kincaid
Cover Art: Margot Pandone on Unsplash
Author Photo: Unknown
Cover Design: Elizabeth Maines McCleavy

Printed in the USA on acid-free paper.
Order online: www.finishinglinepress.com
also available on amazon.com

Author inquiries and mail orders:
Finishing Line Press
P. O. Box 1626
Georgetown, Kentucky 40324
U. S. A.

Table of Contents

To Mrs. Godfrey and to my landlord and landlady

I don't know, but I thought I sensed
a murmur, there, midstream,
and far below me...
My hair began to drip and quick
as I can tell you—quicker—
I had turned into a wave.

Ovid, *Metamorphoses*, V. 774, 813-14

Esther and Willow

This is the pool set halfway between the guesthouse and the main house, built by Mrs. Godfrey in 1941, the year Esther Williams started at MGM. I swim on the diagonal to make a length a little longer. The water's warm where the LA sun has touched it, cool where it floats in shade. I'm taking my first swim in Mrs. Godfrey's pool. My landlord Al says Mrs. Godfrey was one of Esther Williams's understudies. The guesthouse is white, the sky blue, the house at the corner of Esther and Willow. Al says this is a coincidence. I don't believe him. Coincidence is a myth.

David Hockney

Blue denim-colored pool, yellow daylight working on the squiggly ripples, green potted plants on red paving stones, drain distorted by oils on water.

Top step wavy-stamped: credit "Hockney Pools." Inside underwater joke.

I made this up.

Illegal

Al likes me. He says they don't always get someone as unobtrusive as me living in the guesthouse across the pool from them in the main house. He's grateful because the guesthouse is illegal, he doesn't have a permit to rent.

Deirdre

Al doesn't really want the next-door neighbor to know he's converted the garage to a guesthouse, even though next-door remains unoccupied right now. He'd prefer not to give me the neighbor's name or contact info. I want to ask the neighbor about Mrs. Godfrey because he knew her when he was a boy. I want to find her. Al says he thinks her name might have been something like Deirdre.

In the Guesthouse

Skinny white dining table, separating kitchen from living room, perpendicular to a white couch and glass coffee table facing the TV on a white wicker bureau at the end of a queen-sized, blue-covered, un-pillowed bed. Like living in Mrs. Godfrey's swimming pool, same dimensions, blue and white, but dry.

I'm watching all of Esther Williams's movies in hopes of spotting Mrs. Godfrey, her unknown face, her untold name.

Dorinda Clifton

Daughter of director, writer, actor and producer Elmer Clifton. Thirteen movies to her so-called name, including *Annie Get Your Gun*. Al says Dorinda doesn't sound right. He thinks Mrs. Godfrey's name might have been more like Dana, and Mr. Godfrey's name might have been Wayne.

The idea of being un-credited, un-.

Culver City

If you come to the end of Motor Ave., where it stops at Sony Pictures, you can see how the building goes on for blocks. Behind it, once, the original MGM back lots, sound stages, Stage 30, the enormous tank designed for Esther Williams, complete with special effects and underwater dollies. I was on my way to see my friend Jane, ten minutes from Mrs. Godfrey's house. Jane walked me past the old Hollywood fake ante-bellum mansion that had been David Selznick's studio, across the street from the Culver Hotel, once owned by John Wayne, where Judy Garland and the Munchkins stayed. Victor Fleming had only a few short blocks to walk after finishing *Gone with the Wind* at Selznick Studios to take over *The Wizard of Oz* at MGM. 1939. Billy Rose's Aquacade opened at the New York World's Fair. Esther Williams turned eighteen. Jane says her landlady went to high school with Esther Williams. She says people with in-ground pools treat her like dirt because she works at a pool place. When she kept books for the accountant, people treated her with respect.

Bonnie Blue

My best friend, named for Rhett and Scarlett's daughter in *Gone with the Wind*.

Her father grew orchids, pruned trees, trapped rats, took care of the community's indoor swimming pool. The silvery smell of chlorine in his clothes.

Our voices echoed off the undulating walls: Let's float on our backs, point our toes in unison, do backwards somersaults and come up holding hands. Is your father watching?

In our one-piece bathing suits, caps with flapping rubber flowers, adjustable straps under our chins. Bonnie looked just like Esther Williams, same broad torso, same long feet. I had blue hair and a tail.

But on land we both had two legs and braces on our teeth.

Mothers

Where Bonnie lived, on the other side of the woods. Where sometimes I climbed across the low stone wall and waded down the creek to her house. Where she might be sweeping the front steps or washing windows or unmaking beds. When one day Bonnie went to my house to help my mother clean closets, while her mother taught me how to iron sheets. How ironing makes me happy, to make a sheet as smooth as still water.

By the Sea, By the Sea

We went to the beach. My granddaughter said she understood why the waves were quiet: because they worked so hard all night. My grandson said he wanted to go in the deep end. My son-in-law doesn't know who Esther Williams was.

Mansion on the Beach

All that's left of the mansion on the beach is the beach, the ocean, the guesthouse and the pool. When William Randolph Hearst undertook to develop the property for Marion Davies, the water came up very nearly to the guesthouse door. Now it's half a mile away across the sand. How did that happen? Did the ocean somewhere else swallow half a mile of coastline? Some people think the ocean's like a blanket. If one person pulls more of it over to his side of the bed, doesn't the other, uncovered person lie there freezing?

In Marion Davies's Pool

You had just learned to put your head underwater, kick, kick, kick, come up for breath, push the hair every time away from your goggles, little pink fish-eyes, talking, instructing. The pool was tiled with waves and little fishes, sea horses and gold. I loved you. It was like being able to watch you in the womb. Let's blow bubbles underwater, clap hands underwater, touch the bottom with our feet, touch the bottom with our hands, swim to the ladder—you stay there, Granty, let me swim to you, closer, swim to you, farther, swim to you, closer and better and farther and farther—until, little fish, you are, that quick, grown and gone.

Somersault

I showed you how to do a somersault. I pushed your little body in a circle underwater. I said, this is how it feels to do a somersault. Because that's how you learn, by how it feels. The first word Helen Keller ever spoke was *water*.

Lady Guinifever

How she swam underwater, my mother did, underneath the North Pole in her chain mail bathing suit. Once, on a dare, under the Continent, until she rose, like Venus, in a desert oasis, floating with the Bedouin on their shifting seas of sand. She could have gone to the Olympics, of course, like Esther Williams, except for the fact that, in Esther's case, they were cancelled, and except, in my mother's case, you know, in ancient Greece. Every pool, she said, is a flying carpet, blue and magic in the summer sun. It can take you anywhere.

This Is War

Though my mother was nothing if not competitive. She made sure Eleanor Holm got caught for drinking in First Class, sent home from the Olympics in 1936. She saw to it the 1940 Olympics were cancelled so that Esther Williams couldn't win. Well, she said, untying her apron, how could I know it would lead to such a fuss.

Pierce Brothers Westwood Village Memorial Park & Mortuary

Here is the graveyard where Fanny Brice is buried. Here is the graveyard where Fanny Brice, vaudeville comedienne and wife of Billy Rose, is buried. Here is the graveyard where Fanny Brice, vaudeville comedienne and wife of Billy Rose, stolen from her by the scandalous Eleanor Holm, is buried. Here is the graveyard where Fanny Brice, vaudeville comedienne and wife of Billy Rose, stolen from her by the scandalous Eleanor Holm (backstroke champ and star of Billy Rose's 1939 New York World's Fair Aquacade), is buried. Here is the graveyard where Fanny Brice, vaudeville comedienne and wife of Billy Rose, stolen from her by the scandalous Eleanor Holm (backstroke champ and star of Billy Rose's 1939 New York World's Fair Aquacade), whose role was assumed by the young, unassuming Esther Williams at the Golden Gate International Exposition Aquacade (1940), is buried. And where, oh where is Mrs. Godfrey? Alive? Or is she the autumn leaf debris I'm swimming through?

Mickey Rooney

It ain't easy, I'm tellin' ya, smilin' underwater. The water's cold, for one thing, it gets behind your teeth, fills your mouth while you're holdin' your breath or tryin' to breathe through your nose, at the same time you're supposed to be lookin' at the friggin' camera. Esther taught me, though, how to close my throat (like by starting to say "K"), so I could open my mouth without havin' to swallow, sputter, scramble to the surface, make an unmitigated, goddam, idiotic fool of Mickey Rooney.

The Idea of *Mister* Godfrey

To wake at the sound of a splash, to see through the sliding glass doors of the guesthouse: a man in Mrs. Godfrey's pool. Swimming fast, face down, dangling. I miss my husband. The weather's hot in LA for October. It's not Mr. Godfrey, of course. It's Al. Unabashed. He says he's thought it over. Mr. Godfrey's name isn't Wayne. In *Million Dollar Mermaid*, a producer offers Annette Kellerman the lead in *Neptune's Daughter*. His name's also Godfrey. I suppose that's just a coincidence, too?

Film Like Water

Flows. Flickers. Light is everything, immersed, engulfed. Inside it, you dream weightless, willing dreams: you could be anybody, nobody, credited, un-; but when you wake, you harden into matter, every single frame, your one mortality.

The Idea of Being a Wave

Young, beautiful, second from the left. Your feet leave puddles on the pool deck, your hair begins to drip, you dive into the wave you then become. That feeling. No matter what happens the rest of your whole, anonymous, un-credited life.

Dorothy Abbott

"When a person's fated, others go with them." Her one ungrammatical spoken line. Her movies with Esther Williams: *Neptune's Daughter, Take Me Out to the Ball Game*. Also *Words and Music*, with Ann Sothern (1948); *There's No Business Like Show Business*, with Marilyn Monroe (1954). Married handsome Rudy Diaz (1949), one of the first cops to arrive at Marilyn's house the night she died (August 5, 1962). Got my real estate license, Dorothy said in her husky voice, just in case. Prescient. Rudy resigned from the force to take up acting, had an affair with Ann Sothern, left Dorothy flat. She killed herself the day before her birthday (December 15, 1968), nobody seems to know exactly how. She would have been 48. Marilyn was 36.

Un.

Lily

What if Mrs. Godfrey was the stand-in who sank to the bottom of the pool trying to hold up the equipment that checked the color balance of the film? It was new, the equipment, heavy, unwieldy, called the "lily." She was young, inexperienced, eager, unidentified, replaced.

Rapture of the Deep

Esther Williams almost drowned on the set of *Million Dollar Mermaid*.
She laid her pretty head on the pearl of the seashell at the bottom of the
tank and went to sleep.

Esther! Esther! the director shouted into the underwater speaker.
What are you doing! Get your head off that pearl. It's just been painted!

She didn't want to. She was smiling, submerged, an unpainted Botticelli
Venus on the half-shell.

Says she, anybody tells you I didn't do my own stunts is a liar.

LSD

The same way you let yourself fall backwards, blind-folded, into some stranger's arms.

You depend on the doctor (the way you do the director) to keep you safe while you sink into friendly, frightening, vibrant, violent, ravenous, ravishing, unreal, mysterious, musical, (un)clear, turbulent, titillating, simultaneous, spontaneous, unswimmable, undoable, undone, undulating, evermore, nevermore, never more you.

Besides, if Cary Grant suggests you try something, well, you fucking do it!

Converted Triangle

When I get my landlord's next-door neighbor's number from my landlord's wife. When the neighbor says he used to clean Mrs. Godfrey's pool as a kid. When he knows her name but doesn't know where she is. When he says if I find her, he'll surprise her with a Christmas card. When I say sure.

When my friend the genealogist discovers her address, that she's alive and living in the California desert. When I call her. When she says yes, she was Esther Williams's understudy. When she says she just looked like her: B cup, 5'8", 134, brown hair, shape a converted triangle—wide shoulders, slim waist, narrow hips. She stood in. She swam in the chorus. She got no billing. She doesn't care. A long time ago. A good life. When she says her name is Dune.

Pool Party

Our neighbors back home in Edgefield spent all summer putting in a pool. Pink Travertine marble deck, denim blue pool. At the shallow end, a shelf where the water, eighteen inches deep, accommodates two lawn chairs and a beach umbrella, absent tonight when they throw their first pool party. It's late November.

While we eat, the sun sets orange behind the trees at the end of the lawn. The air's cool, not yet cold. The leaves still green, but turning.

At dusk, George takes out his remote. He changes the color of the pool from blue to purple to lime to rose, eight different settings. Somehow he can fill the air with the fragrance of gardenias. He turns on jets set in the marble deck, eight streams of water arching over the pool, like an Esther Williams production number.

Now isn't that me and Bonnie and Esther and Dune swimming synchro under there, slowly rolling, onto our stomachs, onto our backs? There's a word for that gesture. Spinning? Rotation? As in grave? As in planet? Off camera I think the director may be shouting, Esther! Esther! but I can't hear him.

After

After I give the next-door neighbor Mrs. Godfrey's address.

After Christmas.

After I never hear from her again.

After I send her the small ceramic figurine of a kneeling bathing beauty, made in Japan.

After the package is returned to me, unopened.

After she must not have wanted to hear from the next-door neighbor. The word *unpleasant*, the word *surprise*.

After I write to tell her I'm sorry. After I give up trying.

After I put the figurine on my desk.

After Esther Williams dies.

After my hair stops dripping.

NOTES

"I don't know, but"—This translation from Ovid's *Metamorphoses* is by the author.

Esther and Willow—Esther is a real street; Willow is not. Godfrey is a pseudonym.

Somersault—Derived from Provencal *sobra* (above) and *saut* (leap); in old French, *sombresault*; taken from Latin *supra* (over), and *saltus* from *salire* (to leap); settled on its present spelling in mid-16th century. Whether one can technically do a somersault underwater is an unanswered question.

This is War—There was no swimming competition in the original, ancient Greek games, and, of course, there were no female competitors.

Mickey Rooney—See *The Million Dollar Mermaid, An Autobiography*, Esther Williams with Digby Diehl, page 217.

The Idea of *Mister* Godfrey—The producer in *The Million Dollar Mermaid* is not named Godfrey.

Dorothy Abbott—In *Night Has a Thousand Eyes* (1948).

LSD—See *The Million Dollar Mermaid*, pages 12-17.

Pool Party—Edgefield is an historic rural town in western South Carolina.

Award-winning poet **LAUREL BLOSSOM** is the author of two book-length narrative prose poems, *Degrees of Latitude* and *Longevity*, both from Four Way Books. Her earlier books of lyric poetry include *Wednesday: New and Selected Poems*, *The Papers Said* (named a Notable Book of Poetry by *Shelf Unbound*), *What's Wrong*, and a previous chapbook, *Any Minute*. Her 550-line mock epic "Easy Come/Easy Go," was published in *American Poetry Review* in 1976. Her work has appeared in a number of anthologies, including *180 More: Extraordinary Poems for Every Day*, edited by Billy Collins; in national and international journals including *Poetry, Pequod, The Paris Review, Pleiades, xconnect, Deadsnake Apotheosis, Many Mountains Moving, things* (UK), and *Harper's*, among others; and online at friggmagazine.com, BigCityLit.com, Tupelo Quarterly 2, and elsewhere. Her poetry has been nominated for both the Pushcart Prize and the Elliston Prize.

Blossom is the editor of *Splash! Great Writing About Swimming, Many Lights in Many Windows: Twenty Years of Great Fiction and Poetry from The Writers Community, Lovely Village of the Hills: 20th Century Edgefield Poetry,* and *Oxygen* (the poetry of Beatrice Danziger). She served for a number of years on the editorial board of *Heliotrope: a journal of poetry* with co-editors Barbara Elovic, Victoria Hallerman and Susan Sindall.

Blossom has received fellowships from the National Endowment for the Arts, the New York Foundation for the Arts, the Ohio Arts Council, and Harris Manchester College (Oxford University), where she served on the Board of Regents until her retirement. With Helen Chasin, she co-founded The Writers Community, the esteemed writing residency and advanced workshop program of the YMCA National Writer's Voice. Originally founded by Jason Shinder at the West Side YMCA in New York City, Writer's Voice programs continue in Syracuse, New York (under the directorship of Phil Memmer), Billings, Montana (under the directorship of Corby Skinner), and Detroit, Michigan (under the directorship of M.L. Liebler).